CHILDREN DID YOU KNOW
SANTA BELIEVES

Happy Reading,
Sharon Kizziah-Holmes

Written by

SHARON KIZZIAH-HOLMES

Illustrated by

CARLOS LEMOS

Kids Book Press
An imprint of
A & S Publishing – A & S Holmes, Inc.

ISBN-13: 978-0692599532
ISBN-10: 0692599533

Dedication

This book goes out to all of my grandchildren, great grandchildren and to my nieces and nephews.

Keep your faith in God. Turn to Him for guidance and you will always have someone to look up to.

I love each and every one of you!

Acknowledgments

I'd like to thank Carlos Lemos for all of his hard work. You do an awesome job, my friend. Thank you for putting in the extra time to get the illustrations done so quickly. You're the best!

Norma, my good friend, there is so much I wouldn't be able to do without you. You've always been there for me when I need you, not only as a BFF, but as my editor. Thank you for that! I love you.

To my husband, thank you for having faith in me and for always standing by me. Your encouragement keeps me going.
You are my love forever!

Ho, ho, ho! Hi, my name is Kris Kringle, but you probably know me better as Santa Claus. I'd like to tell you a story. You see, during the Christmas season there are symbols all around us that tell a tale; it's just that, most of us don't know what they are. Today, I'd like to teach you the meaning of these symbols..."The Symbols of True Christmas."

At Christmas time, gifts are under the tree, carolers sing in the yard and family and friends gather to share turkey dinner and enjoy each other's company. Do you know what we are really celebrating? It's Jesus' birthday! What a joyful occasion.

Let's start with the Christmas tree. This is a mighty Fir tree. This tree remains green year round. It shows the eternal hope of mankind. If you'll notice, all of its needles point toward the sky. The Fir tree is a symbol that our thoughts should turn toward heaven.

The glowing star that hangs on the tree was a heavenly sign many years ago. God promised us a Savior and the star is the sign that he kept that promise. It led the wise men to the baby Jesus the night of his birth.

The shepherd's crook is signified by the candy cane.
To bring back a sheep that has strayed, the shepherd
will hook the crook of the staff around the sheep's
neck then gently guide it back to the flock.
Therefore, the candy cane is an emblem meaning
we are our brother's keeper. We should help them
find their way. Not only that, but the white strip of
the candy cane represents Jesus' purity, the
red stripe symbolizes His blood.

You see the candle that burns on the table? It's a symbol of the light of the world. When we see it, we should remember God. He who displaces the darkness. In other words, He takes darkness away.

The fruit in the basket in the kitchen symbolizes the twelve Fruits of the Holy Spirit. What are they? Why, they are Peace, Patience, Goodness, Long-Suffering, Mildness, Faith, Modesty, Purity, Chastity, Love and Kindness.

On the door hangs a wreath. It's the symbol
of love and reminds us that love is a
continuous circle that never ends.

KRIS KRINGLE

SANTA

And look, there's an ornament on the tree that resembles me! I am the symbol of the good will and generosity we share during the Christmas season. I'm sometimes called as Saint Nicholas.

ST. NICK

Did you know that the holly leaf is the symbol of the crown of thorns Jesus wore when they crucified him, and the red berries represent his blood? It's true. The holly plant symbolizes immortality.

The gifts under the tree are symbols of the
ultimate gift God gave us. John 3:16 - For God so
loved the world, that he gave his only begotten Son,
that whosoever believeth in Him should not perish,
but have everlasting life.

You'll notice the beautiful angel that sits atop the Christmas tree. She is the symbol of the angel that sang out the magnificent news of the Savior's birth...Glory to God in the highest, peace on earth good will toward men...

The bell that sits on the mantel rings like a bell that hangs from a sheep's neck. It jingles to warn the shepherd when a sheep is lost. It symbolizes guidance to help mankind return to God's flock of children.

What about the yummy gingerbread people Mom creates and designs for you? They are the same color as the earth. This is to remind us that God created Adam from dust in the Garden of Eden. God created all of us.

I, Santa Claus, will be here for you every Christmas,  but please don't make me the center of the season, for I am only a servant of the One that is truly the center of the celebration. I bow down to worship Him, our Lord, our God and Savior, Jesus Christ.

I'll say goodbye for now, but I wish you
a happy holiday season. I'll see you next year.
Remember, now, Jesus IS the reason for the season.

Ho! Ho! Ho!

MERRY CHRISTMAS!

About the Author

Sharon Kizziah-Holmes

I live in the beautiful Ozarks with my husband and two Cocker Spaniels, Dude and Lacy. I have seventeen grandkids and two great grands...that's right, I'm too young, I know... =) However, I love each and every one of them with all my heart, and wouldn't change a thing.

My interest in writing novels came in the early 1990's. A friend suggested we write a book together, so I took her up on it. I joined writing groups and a whole new world opened up for me. I'm still a member of many writing groups. I absolutely love writing, editing, publishing and teaching the basics of writing to others.

My first children's book was written with other authors. Thanks to Michael and Betty Edging for including me in the Camouflage Santa Claus endeavor. That is what inspired me to write 'Children Did You Know, Santa Believes'.

Be sure to get your 'Children Did You Know, Santa Believes' coloring book!

Coming in the spring of 2016, 'Children Did You Know, the Easter Bunny Believes', also with companion coloring book.

Happy Reading and Merry Christmas!

Sharon Kizziah-Holmes

About the Illustrator

Carlos Lemos

Carlos is a freelance illustrator, cartoonist and caricaturist. He started his career in 2006, then in 2010 he became a Visual Art teacher, doing workshops for high schools and colleges.

In 2014 he started an Atelier about comics and caricatures. He makes presentations in Uruguay and Argentina. The workshops also include learning about the creative process.

Over the years, Carlos has illustrated over thirty children's books for people from around the world. Some of his comics include:

"Verano". an anthology with a summer theme.

"Grimorilo do Plata", a dark themed graphic novel.

"Crononautas", a young adult sci-fi graphic novel.

"Carpincho", a historical web comic to the project Ceibal (one computer per child of the public education in his country) www.bandasorientales.com.uy/historietas/carpincho/ and freelance comics for individuals.

He lives in the capital city of Uruguay, Montevideo, with the love of his life and their daughter. He enjoys spending time on the beach with his family, and though he loves his work, Carlos is most proud of being a father.

Made in the USA
San Bernardino, CA
19 September 2017